T0165503

# The Designer's Wardrobe

## Seven Wardrobe Essentials for Christian Living

### SHELLEY WISE REININGER

WESTBOW
PRESS
A DIVISION OF THOMAS NELSON

Scripture taken from the King James Version of the Bible.

WestBow Press books may be ordered through booksellers or by contacting:

WestBow Press
A Division of Thomas Nelson
1663 Liberty Drive
Bloomington, IN 47403
www.westbowpress.com
1-(866) 928-1240

ISBN: 978-1-4497-3035-2 (e)
ISBN: 978-1-4497-3036-9 (sc)
ISBN: 978-1-4497-3037-6 (hc)

Library of Congress Control Number: 2011919672

Printed in the United States of America

WestBow Press rev. date: 11/17/2011

To my wonderful husband and best friend, John, who made this book possible by his continual love, guidance, and gentle prodding.

# Contents

# Acknowledgments

A special thanks to my cousin Jackie Voison who, with heart-wrenching clarity, wrote down her son Christopher's life story.

A heart of indebtedness to the long-term care facility Go Ye Village and Jolly in Tahlequah, Oklahoma, for their endearing and loving care of my precious Uncle Wally.

A special appreciation to my Aunt Margaret and Uncle Donald who helped me with their daughter-in-law Jean's story and who persevered through assisting in editing my project.

A special appreciation to my Aunt Lee, technically my first cousin once removed, who painstakingly also assisted in the editing of my project.

A lifetime of gratitude to my parents who gently reared me by example and not with an iron fist, who tenderly pushed me forward with no expectations, and who have fervently loved me for who I am.

A deep appreciation to all of my family members who continually give me the canvas of examples of people who wear Christ through my eyes. I am so honored to be a part of such an amazing family.

# Foreword

This study was written primarily for the ladies of the WOW (Women of the Word) Sunday school class who join me in a Sunday morning Bible study at First Baptist Church in Rochelle, Illinois. Their interaction has proved invaluable to me.

This series of lessons focuses on essential elements of a woman's spiritual wardrobe. Follow along as we study these wardrobe essentials with the challenge to choose them with modesty and thrift and at the same time glorify our life in Christ. Also challenge yourself to answer the questions throughout each lesson to reconfirm God's challenge to us to wear our new garments. Use the "Thoughts to Ponder" section at the end of each lesson to help make personal application to your own life.

# Lesson 1: The New Wardrobe

*"Therefore if any man be in Christ, he is a new creature: old things are passed away; behold all things are become new"* (1 Corinthians 5:17).

I was reared in a Christian home and went to church most of my life. In vacation Bible school (VBS) one summer, around my sixth grade year, I was persuaded about my need to be saved. During the preaching time, any VBS kids were asked to come forward if they wanted to be saved. Since a bunch of kids went forward, I went forward at the same time to be saved. A lady took all of us into a big circle, shared some Scripture, and then prayed. I was given the book of John, and the lady told us we were saved.

As I began my teenage years, I struggled with an assurance that I was saved. I believed that I was a sinner, that Jesus died on the cross for my sins, and that He arose from the grave. I believed Jesus was the Son of God. I also knew the Bible said if "thou shalt confess with thy mouth the Lord Jesus and believe in thine heart that God hath raised him from the dead, thou shalt be saved" (Romans 9:10). I also knew the Bible said that whosoever shall call upon the Lord shall be saved (Romans 9:13). However, that was the problem. I couldn't remember if I called on the Lord and actually confessed my sins back in VBS, and I didn't remember asking Jesus into my heart.

I allowed the following items to make me think I was saved:

- going forward in a service;

- a lady sharing Scripture and praying;

- a lady telling me I was saved; and

- receiving the book of John.

I knew as a teenager that none of these things had saved me, nor would they give me eternal life with God. I just couldn't remember anywhere in the VBS scenario having personal time with God about my need to be saved, talking with Him, and confessing my sin to Him.

One evening our youth group watched a film depicting what would happen at the rapture and what it would be like to go to hell for anyone not saved when he or she died. It was terrifying! That night, as I lay in my bed looking up at the stars, I was very afraid to close my eyes for fear I would wake up in hell. Then I decided to resolve this lack of assurance about being saved. I don't know what day or time it was, but I do know that I told Jesus I was a sinner on my way to hell. I asked Him to forgive me of my sin and come and live in my heart. At that point of salvation, I began to develop a new wardrobe and an extreme makeover began in my life.

An extreme makeover is only possible through the shed blood of Jesus Christ and the "continuing housework of the indwelling Holy Spirit."[1]

1. According to Romans 3:23, we are all_____.

2. According to Romans 6:23, we are all_____to die.

3. What did Christ do for us, according to Romans 5:8?

4. What two things must we do to be saved, according to Romans 10:9?

5. According to 1 John 1:9, we must acknowledge what?

6. According to Romans 10:13, who must do what? What then will happen?

When we acknowledge and confess our sins, God cancels our punishment of hell because we acknowledge that Jesus Christ went to the cross on our behalf.

7. After salvation, what does 1 John 5:10–12 say people have?

8. What happened the moment we believed, according to John 5:24? What else do people have the moment they believe?

Becoming a Christian doesn't mean we are perfect. We are spiritual babies and need to grow in grace.

9. According to Philippians 1:6, what does God do in our lives?

## THOUGHTS TO PONDER

- Was there a time in my life when I realized I was a sinner on my way to hell?

- Do I believe that Jesus Christ died on the cross for my sins and that He rose again the third day?

- Was there a time in my life when I verbally confessed my sin to Christ, asked Him to forgive me of my sin, and asked Him to come and live in my heart?

If you have never been saved and would like to today, just talk to God. Tell Him you know that you are a sinner on your way to hell and you believe that He died on the cross for your sins. Ask God to forgive you of your sins and to come and live in your heart. If you just asked God to save you, please e-mail me at sdreininger@yahoo.com so I can rejoice and pray for you.

# Lesson 2: The Old Wardrobe

*"Mortify therefore your members which are upon the earth ... and put on the new man"* (Colossians 3:5, 10).

After our extreme makeover of salvation, we are told to put off the old man and wear the new man. In order to put off the old man, we must discard the filthy garments of our old, sinful lives the same way a person removes his or her dirty clothes at the end of the day.

While I was working as a summer youth counselor at Camp Joy, in Whitewater, Wisconsin, a youth pastor told the following true story that is a great example of choosing whether to discard our old garments of sin after we're saved or to continue to wear our old garments of sinful ways after being saved.

Two teenage sisters who had professed salvation, Linda and Susie, came from one of the most stable and precious families in the youth pastor's church.

Linda had made different choices than Susie did. Linda chose to rebel against her parents and by her senior year in high school gave her parents major discipline problems. Linda met Jim, who had just been saved and was on fire for the Lord. He was showing signs of spiritual growth within the youth group. Jim and Linda began dating, and Linda started showing an interest in godly things. Meanwhile, Jim fell deeply in love. However, Linda soon became tired of serving God, dating Jim, and dealing with her family. Linda chose to run away from home to get away from Jim and her severe family conflicts. Linda became involved in a gang, which led to drug abuse. One day Jim, depressed about losing Linda, opened the door to find her standing on the porch. She had come to his house to give back his class ring. As Jim stood there trying to persuade Linda to change her mind, he reached for a pistol and shot Linda seven times; then he turned the gun on himself.

The pastor stated, "Two enterprising young people, both with credentials from a fundamental Bible-preaching church, lay in a pool of their own blood. The cause of their death was sin: unrestrained, undisciplined life; rebellion against the Lord and against parents; and the inability to forgive and be forgiven."

The other girl in the family, Susie, grew up in the same environment. Susie faced the same family traumas and pressures that Linda did.

1. Susie, as a seventh grader, surrendered her life to the mission field.

2. Susie offered a consistent testimony in her youth group.

3. She was a faithful helper with the bus ministry as a teen.

4. She memorized more Scripture than any young person in the history of the church.

5. Susie was an honor roll student and worked at a job while attending high school.

6. She graduated from a Christian college with a degree in missions.[2]

## TAKING OFF THE OLD WARDROBE

In the story above, even though Linda claimed to have accepted Jesus Christ as her personal Savior, she did not choose to take off the old garments of sin. She enjoyed her contrary, rebellious, self-centered life. Linda chose to leave her old wardrobe of sinfulness on and allowed the old, nasty garments of sin to continue to rule in her life. She chose the old, nasty garments over the new wardrobe of Christlikeness and allowing God to control her life. That sinful life that Linda chose became a poor influence on her new boyfriend who was a young Christian.

The word *mortify* in verse five of Colossians 3 and the phrase "putting off the old man" in verse eight of the same chapter mean bringing the old sinful nature under control and treating the old nature as though it were dead. The words are considered aorist imperative, which means both are considered a simple action and not a continual action.[3] Therefore, we are expected, as new creatures in Christ, to take off our old garments one time, to treat them as though they are dead, and never to put the old garments back on again.

## OLD WARDROBE SIN OF SENSUAL DESIRES

God loves you too much to allow you to mess up your life with sensual sins. We need to be zealous for God's honor by putting these evil desires to death. According to 1 Corinthians 6:18–20, we are to flee sexual immorality. Any form of illicit sexual behavior includes a mind filled with suggestive thoughts, always wanting quick fulfillment to satisfy your selfish desires, evil desires that are motivated by the sinful nature, and the sin of always wanting more than you have. We are not just to put these sensual desires aside, wound them, explain them away, rationalize them, or play around with them. Instead we are to kill them.

1.   According to Colossians 3:5, list the words used to describe sensual sins that we are to put off.

## OLD WARDROBE SIN OF THE TONGUE

It has been said the tongue is one of the most exercised muscles of our body. It has been estimated that in a typical week, the average person will speak enough words to fill a five-hundred-page book. However, for the Christian, the use of the tongue must be a matter of careful forethought and discipline.

In Colossians 3:8, we are told to put off these sins of the tongue. We are to strip off, or to take off like you take off your clothes, these sins of the tongue. These sins of the tongue include deep, smoldering resentment internalized, flaming bitterness externalized, evil speaking, slander, filthy talk, and lying. All of the words listed in Colossians 3:8 involve some type of communication, whether verbal or nonverbal. They are also based on some type of selfishness. The sin of selfishness has consumed us from the time the first sin was committed in the garden of Eden until this present day.

"If any man among you seem to be religious and bridleth not his tongue, but deceiveth his own heart, this man's religion is in vain" (James 1:26). It is a deception for any of us to think that Jesus can be Lord over our life without also becoming Lord over our tongue.

2.  Define *putting off.*

3.  According to Colossians 3:8, list the words used to describe the sin of the tongue.

4.  In item three, the sins listed are what part of the body?

5.   According to Ephesians 4:31, what are we to put away?

6.   According to Ephesians 4:29–30, what does filthy communication do to the Holy Spirit?

7.   Define *grieve*.

Dr. Dave Jaspers, president of Maranatha Baptist Bible College, reminds us that "you can only grieve someone who loves you, but a stranger you will only make angry." People may dislike us and get angry with us when we sin; however, as a Christian, we don't make the Lord angry. We grieve Him when we sin because he loves us and wants us to be more like Christ.

## OLD WARDROBE SIN OF SELFISHNESS

In Genesis we read that Eve was tempted by the fruit and was influenced by the serpent, who convinced her that if she ate of the fruit she would become wise. So Eve disregarded the warnings not to eat of that particular tree because she wanted to become wise. Because of her selfish disobedience, sin had entered the world.

The degree to which individuals overcome selfishness determines the success and happiness of all their interpersonal relationships.[4] Selfish people usually think first, last, and always of themselves. Selfishness appears most clearly in their conversation and conduct, which is primarily about them. Selfishness can be extremely destructive to a marriage. When you are considering a marriage partner, carefully examine his or her treatment of others, especially family members. Showing consideration of others is an indication of future marital harmony. People are not old enough for matrimony until they are unselfish enough to think more of someone else's needs and desires than their own.[5]

8.   In the following passages, who was selfish and what did they want?

Genesis 3:6

Genesis 4:1–8

Isaiah 14:12–14

## DISCARDING THE OLD GARMENTS OF SIN

If we are to have real victory over our old nature or the "old garment," we must give Jesus the total right to rule in our lives. Although as a Christian we have the Holy Spirit living in us, He hasn't necessarily been given the right to rule in every area of our lives. Our old nature or the old garment is not happy about our salvation because it has enjoyed the unchallenged influence in our lives since we were born. The old garment won't give up this deep-rooted power without a fight. This process of defeating the old nature can take a lifetime.

The place that we are to be continually working on our makeover is inside us, in our heart. Our heart is the center of the entire man: the inner person; the seat of desires, feelings, impulses, and passions; the seat of conscience. Our heart is the totality of us.

9.  Define *heart.*

10.  According to 1 Samuel 16:7b, what is the difference between how other people see us and how God sees us?

11.  According to Proverbs 4:23, what are we to guard and why?

12.  According to Philippians 1:6, what is God doing continually?

The "Sons of Thunder" have given us an example of how we can attempt to discard our old garments of sin, choose to walk with Jesus, be taught by Jesus, yet still act and react out of human rationalization rather than by the principles by which He told us to live.[6]

13. Read Luke 9:51–56 about the Sons of Thunder and then answer the following questions:

- Who was upset and why?

- What did they want to do?

- What was Jesus's response?

## THE STRONGHOLD OF SATAN

Satan will do everything in his power to exploit our old nature or the old garment. If Satan can get you into a place of spiritual ineffectiveness, you will no longer be in a position where God can use you.[7] Daily we need to give our lives to the Lord and rest in His promises so that our old nature will be forced to bow the knee and submit to God. To have daily victory over our old nature, we must continually put our minds under the control of the Lord.

"And be not conformed to this world: but be ye transformed by the renewing of your mind, that ye may prove what is that good, and acceptable and perfect will of God" (Romans 12:2).

14. How do the following verses describe Satan?

2 Corinthians 11:14

John 8:44

Eph 6:12

1 Peter 5:8

## THE POWER OF GOD IN OUR LIVES

15. According to the following verses, how is our God described?

Psalms 28:1a

Psalms 62:2, 6

Psalms 94:22

Psalms 71:3b

16. What do the following verses say God will do if we remain faithful and true to Him?

John 16:13

Psalms 145:14

Psalms 145:18

Psalms 37:24

Deuteronomy 33:27

Isaiah 41:10

Psalms 31:23


Psalms 37:28


2 Timothy 4:18


Because of what Christ did on the cross and because of His ongoing redemptive work in our lives, we are being made new: restored, changed, transformed. We must "continually ask the Holy Spirit to make us aware of the snares created by our human weaknesses and of our own deceitful desires and place them in God's hands."[8]

17. What do the following verses say we have in Christ?

Romans 8:37


1 Corinthians 15:57


2 Corinthians 2:14

Ephesians 6:10

It isn't a matter of working toward a victory but of walking in a victory already secured by the power of the Lord. In Christ we have already won the battle.[9]

18. List below the promises we can claim

1 Corinthians 10:13

Philippians 4:7

Hebrews 13:5–6

## WEARING THE NEW WARDROBE

In Colossians 3:10 "is renewed" means to renew, renovate, to change from a carnal being to a Christian. It is also in the present passive participle, which means it is a continuous, repeated action of the subject, which is "the new woman."[10] "The new woman receives the verb "is renewed" in knowledge. When we accept Christ as our personal Savior, our goal should be continually to strive to yield to Christ. We then begin to wear the new garments, which are continually being renewed with divine knowledge after the likeness of God who created us. We are continually striving to be more like Christ, to wear Christ.

In the story at the beginning of this lesson, Susie made the choice of taking off the old garments and putting on the new garments. Susie made a choice to serve God, obey the Scriptures, and to wear Christ.

The Bible tells us in Romans 13:4 that we are to "put ye on the Lord Jesus Christ," in Galatians 3:27 to "put on Christ," in Ephesians 4:23–25 to "put on the new man," and in Ephesians 6:11 "to put on the whole armor of God."

As Christians, the Bible instructs us to clothe, to adorn, to cover, to equip, and to bear ourselves with Christ. We are to put off the old garments and we are to put on Christ.

19. As Christians, according to Isaiah 61:10, what has God clothed us with?

We will keep our priorities straight if we constantly put our eyes and emphasis upon the clothing of our souls.[11] Ryrie says that we should "become in experience what we already are by God's grace. The Christian is risen with Christ let him (her) exhibit that new life to others."[12]

20. Paul describes something in Romans 7:15–24. What is constantly happening in our lives?

Remember our old nature is not working on our behalf or working for our benefit. The old nature is continually striving to be in control of our lives, just as Paul described it in Romans 7:15–8:1. God has given us a free will; therefore we need to be daily challenged to build a relationship with the Lord. In so doing, we will be able to remove those sinful habits, wrong attitudes, and impure motives by asking God to give us the power to wear Christ in our lives. We then will overcome this old nature because Christ will give us the conquest.

## THOUGHTS TO PONDER

- Am I a Linda or a Susie?

- Am I striving to build a relationship with the Lord?

- Do I have sinful habits, wrong attitudes, or impure motives that I have not given up?

- Do I have victory over sensual sins?

- Do I have victory over sins of my tongue?

- Do I have victory over sins of selfishness or impure motives?

- Does God have the victory in my life or have I allowed Satan to continue to destroy me?

- Have I asked God to give me the power to wear Christ in my life?

# Lesson 3: The LBD of Mercy

*"Put on therefore ... bowels of mercies"* (Colossians 3:10).

The LBD, also known as the *Little Black Dress,* originated in the 1920s. It is considered essential for every lady's wardrobe because it never looks out of place for any occasion, is versatile, a perfect canvas for accessories, and will never go out of fashion. Mercy is the *LBD* of our Christian wardrobe, as it is an essential element for every situation because it is never out of place and very versatile.

One snowy New Years' Day morning, my family awakened to about two feet of snow and bitterly cold temperatures. My dad was sitting at the kitchen table looking outside at the beautiful new-fallen snow and noticed near the steps to the house a glove lying in the snow. My dad looked again and the glove was gone but there was a coat instead. Out of curiosity my dad braved the cold temperatures and went outside to find a young man almost frozen to death in the snow, desperately trying to get up the stairs to the house for help. My dad immediately got him into the house and my mom and dad worked carefully and feverishly to get his body temperature back to normal.

It appeared the young man was so intoxicated the night before that he thought he was on the road to his house, got stuck in the snow in my dad's driveway, and fell asleep. In the morning when he awoke, he saw he was close to a house and crawled to the house for help. The young man survived the ordeal and years later expressed to my brother that he knew my mom and dad had saved his life that day. The experience caused the young man to reevaluate his life, and he then accepted Jesus Christ as his personal Savior. This young man's life was saved because my parents showed him mercy, and his soul was saved because of God's unending love and mercy to him.

The LBD of mercy works with every situation—and is essential to every wardrobe. The phrase "bowels of mercy" is focused on the center of tenderness and compassion, sorrow for the sufferings of another, and an urge to help involving thoughts and actions.

"Bowels of mercy" is a form of love determined by the state or condition of its object. The state is one of suffering and need, even when the person may be unworthy or ill deserving.

## CHRIST'S MERCY

From a human standpoint, the young man in the story above didn't really do anything to deserve my parent's special attention and care. He was a dirty, drunken stranger who changed the course of my family's itinerary for the day. He had interrupted our ability to eat a quiet breakfast, shovel the driveway, and even get to church. However because of my parents' love for the Lord and their desire and compassion to help a stranger in need, that day became the turning point for this young man's eternal destiny. Because my parents showed mercy on this young man and saved his life, this young man began to understand more completely Christ's mercy for us, and he asked Jesus Christ to save His soul. After hearing his testimony years later, I too was challenged to continually wear mercy. We cannot be merciful to others unless we understand the mercy God has for us.

1.   In the following verses, describe the Lord's mercy.

Psalms 25:6

Psalms 86:5

Psalms 103:17

Psalms 106:1

Psalms 108:4

Lamentations 3:22


Titus 3:5


2. In Lesson 2 we studied Luke 9:52–56 about the Sons of Thunder. What was wrong with the disciples' response to the situation?


3. According to Matt 5:7, how do we obtain mercy?


Being merciful is described as having benevolent compassion involving thought and action.[13] Mercy is also explained as an internal attitude that results in an external action. Mercy demands a deliberate effort of the mind and will and a deliberate identification with another person.[14]

In Mark 6:17–44 is the story of John the Baptist, Herod Antipas, and Herodias. John proceeds to tell Herod Antipas not to marry Herodias because it is "unlawful for you to have your brother's wife" (verse eighteen). Herodias fights with John the Baptist and wants to kill him, but Herod the Great hides John in the prison away from Herodias. A birthday party comes up for Herod the Great, and his granddaughter Salome treats her grandfather to a dance for his birthday present. According to Mark 6:22, Herod the Great is pleased and tells his granddaughter that he will give her whatever she wants. Salome goes to her mother Herodias and asks her opinion on what she should ask her grandfather to provide.[15] Herodias tells Salome to request John the Baptist's head. John the Baptist is murdered and in Mark 6:29–30 the disciples go and get the body of John and bury him.

In the midst of Jesus's mourning for his cousin John the Baptist, Jesus showed mercy on people gathering around Him. Jesus chose to spend time with people who needed to hear the gospel. Even though He was very tired and hungry and the disciples wanted the people to go away, Christ wanted to feed the people. During a time of anguish for Christ and the disciples, Christ performed the miracle of feeding the five thousand with five loaves and two fish.

4. According to the above story, what should you do when you are the most discouraged, downtrodden, disappointed, hopeless, and sad?

People who inspire others are those who see invisible bridges at the end of dead-end streets. [16]

## BIBLICAL EXAMPLE OF MERCY

The following Bible story in Luke 10:30–35 tells of a Jewish man who was robbed and beaten up on his way down to Jericho. There were three individuals who passed by the injured man: a Samaritan who was despised by Jews because of their mixed Gentile blood, a priest who took care of the sanctuary of God, and a Levite who was a gatekeeper in the temple. One of the men showed mercy on the Jewish man, and the other two did not show mercy. Sadly not the one you would expect.

5.  Describe the scene in Luke 10 by answering the following questions.

Who is robbed and beaten up?

Who first passes by and what does he do?

Who passes by next and what two things does he do?

Who passes by next and what does he do?

6.  Who showed an internal response that resulted in an external action?

7.  Who showed an external response but nothing internal?

8. According to 1 John 3:17, if "bowels of compassion" are not displayed in your life, what is the condition of your heart?

## SHOWING MERCY

9. According to Proverbs 22:9, what does it mean to have a bountiful eye?

With every encounter, make it your aim that people are better off having been in your presence. [17] Don't wait to be encouraged: step out of your comfort zone and be an encourager.

The following represent someone possessing a "self-sacrificing love."

- Willingness to go the distance for someone in trouble

- Attitude of loving compassion for the needy

- Availability to help in practical, tangible ways

- Helping people feel needed and important

- Simply touching, just being present

- Hugging, smiling, greeting (with someone's name)[18]

10. In Luke 10:27, what are we commanded to do?

Your neighbors are people in your path needing your help. They are in need whether they brought it upon themselves or not. Author Elizabeth George challenges us to regularly place ourselves before God and let Him grow in us, strengthen us, and transform us.[19] While doing that, we will have more to give to our neighbor, even during difficult times. Elizabeth George also reminds us that the impact of our ministry to people will be in direct proportion to the time we spend away from people and with God.[20]

11. According to Joshua 20:2, 4, just like the Old Testament cities, we should be a place of what?

Do we provide a place where broken people have time to recover from their wounds and build up their self-esteem? Our local church should be one of those places; however, as author Charles Swindol so aptly stated, Christianity may be "like a mighty army but we often handle our troops in a weird way. We're the only outfit I've ever heard of who shoots their wounded."[21]

12. According to the following verses, what is the result of giving mercy or not giving mercy?

• Proverbs 11:17

- Matthew 5:7

- James 2:13

## QUESTIONS TO PONDER

- To whom does a Christian turn when something embarrassing or scandalous happens?

- Who cares enough to listen when we cry?

- Who affirms us when we feel rotten?

- Who will close their mouths and open their hearts?

- Who will embrace us with understanding, even though we deserve a swift kick in the pants?

- Who will give us time to heal from our mistakes without quoting verses, without giving us a CD/tape of some sermon to listen to?

- Who will let us heal without telling a bunch of other Christians so they can "pray more intelligently"?[22]

- Do I possess mercy? **Do I wear Christ**

# Lesson 4: The Classic Pump of Kindness

*"Put on therefore ... Kindness"* (Colossians 3:10).

The lady's classic pump is a true fashion classic, designed to be worn with almost anything and one that will see you through many types of occasions. The *classic pump of kindness* is also essential for any type of occasion.

My brother Kurt accepted Christ as His personal Savior at an early age, and he grew into a love for the sciences and how they fit into the Bible, God's plan for us, and our universe. He received undergraduate and graduate degrees in geology and paleontology, became a scientist, became a college and seminary professor, established friendships with Creationists throughout the world, taught at the Institute for Creation Research in the summers, and helped design the Creation Museum in Ohio. Kurt also developed hobbies in astronomy, taxidermy, photography, spelunking, and genealogy. Kurt has also been working to improve the science curriculum in schools today, has written books on creation, and has been highlighted in magazine articles throughout the years, including *Newsweek*. Kurt is a busy man, yet he loves life to the fullest and is continually challenged by God's Word and the beautiful universe God has given us.

Kurt's accomplishments have always seemed to come easy for him; however, life for my brother has not always been an easy road. As a child I remember Kurt being ridiculed in the grade school playground because he was so intelligent and kind of geekish. He was scorned in high school for the same thing, yet he never let it stop him from continuing his goals God had for his life. Kurt was defied by Christians who thought it was unacceptable for him to go to the University of Chicago and Harvard University because he was a Christian. Kurt was contested by his evolutionist professors because they knew that he stood for the Lord and his belief in the inspired Word of God. Kurt was opposed in seminars across America by the unsaved and saved alike regarding his stand for the Word of God. However, I have never known my brother to say an unkind word to anyone regardless of how he was treated or disputed. My brother has always listened with his heart and has drawn people to the Lord because of his kindness. His unsaved professors developed a strong bond with my brother, and, despite having different beliefs they determined that Kurt would continue his work. Today my brother has made a tremendous impact in the lives of thousands of people, because Kurt is the definition of wearing the kindness of Christ no matter what situation he has endured.

*Kindness* is known in the Greek as *chrestotes* and is defined as the following:

- Moral excellence in character or demeanor

- Tender heart

- Nurturing spirit

- Tender concern for others

- Grace that pervades the whole nature, mellowing all that would be harsh and austere

- Descriptive of one's disposition and doesn't necessarily entail acts of goodness

- Prevailing aspect of your nature[23]


## CHRIST'S KINDNESS

The word for *kindness* is interchangeable with mercy, goodness, loyalty, and faithfulness, but most of all steadfast love. Kindness is the visible action of love directed toward others even when they don't deserve it. As in the testimony of my brother Kurt, he endured much scoffing and mocking for his stand for the Lord, yet he continued to show kindness.

Christ is the ultimate example of kindness in His tender heart and concern He has shown toward others through the centuries.

1. Whom in the following Scripture did Christ have a tender heart toward?

Genesis 21:14–19

Exodus 3:7

Matthew 9:36

Matthew 14:14

Matthew 15:22–28

Matthew 20:29–34

Luke 7:12–14

Luke 19:41

John 20:1–18

## SHOWING KINDNESS

Remember kindness is your compassionate nature—not necessarily the act of goodness. God wants us to have a disposition of "tenderheartedness" and a spirit eager to nurture. [24]

2.  What did Job discover about his friends in Job 16:2?




Sometimes we have to experience misunderstanding from unsympathetic friends in order to learn how to minister to others.[25] The best way to help discouraged and hurting people is to listen with our heart. Listening with our heart is defined as being comforting, soothing, and attending closely

3.  According to 2 Corinthians 1:3–4, what is our responsibility when we have been comforted by God?




God doesn't comfort us to make us comfortable but to make us comforters. God's comfort is never given; it is always loaned.[26] In Galatians 5:22, the Greek word for *gentleness* is *chrestotes*[27], which is the same word used as the word *kindness* in Colossians.

4.  In 2 Corinthians 6:3–6, Paul uses chrestotes as a quality we should have when we are doing what?

5.  Define what it means to minister.

6.  The following verses contain the Greek word chrestotes for the word *kindness*. Describe the subject of chrestotes in each verse.

    Romans 2:4

    2 Corinthians 6:6

    Galatians 5:22

    Ephesians 2:7

    Titus 3:4

Some people saw Jesus during His forty days between His resurrection and His ascension. Jesus had the opportunity to tell a few very special people "I'm Alive!" because of His chrestotes. In the following story in the book of Luke, Mary Magdalene met Jesus. Mary experienced an extreme makeover and she owed

Jesus her life and her sanity because of His kindness or chrestotes to her.[28]

7.   In Luke 8:2 what happened to Mary Magdalene?

- According to Luke, what then did Mary do?

- According to Matt 27:56, what did Mary witness?

- According to Matt 27:57–61, what did Mary see?

- Mary missed Jesus and her heart was tender. According to John 20:11–18, what did Mary experience?

- Jesus appeared to Mary and, according to John 20:18, because of Jesus' *chrestotes* what did He do for Mary?

We find in the Scriptures the description of Jesus's brothers. It appears they did not accept Jesus as Savior until after His crucifixion. Jesus loved his brothers even though they rejected Him during His earthly ministry. We see in the following verses that the brothers eventually believe in Jesus as the Messiah. Out of Christ's tenderness came belief.

*Chrestotes* is the tender concern for others. It has nothing to do with weakness or lack of conviction; rather it is the genuine desire of a believer to treat others gently, just as the Lord treats them.[29]

8.  In Matthew 13:55–56, we learn about Jesus's family.

    •  Who were Jesus's brothers?

    •  According to John 7:5, what do we know about Jesus's brothers?

    •  In 1 Corinthians 15:7, we learn that Jesus appears to whom after his resurrection? And Why?

    •  According to Acts 1:12–14, who in Jesus's family was in the room waiting for the Holy Spirit to come?

QUESTIONS TO PONDER

- Do I treat others as I wish to be treated by them and as God has treated me?

- Do I demonstrate genuine concern for others?

- Am I thoughtful, considerate, and alert to the needs of others?

- Do I have in my Christian wardrobe kindness that will see me through any type of situation? **Am I wearing Christ?**

# Lesson 5: The Hat of Humbleness of Mind

*"Put on therefore ... humbleness of mind"* (Colossians 3:10).

T oday the hat is worn for necessity and for fashion and can accessorize any outfit. The lady's hat was originally designed to show modesty and to protect her from the sin of vanity. The *hat of humbleness of mind* is essential for the Christian Wardrobe because it keeps us from being prideful and unproductive.

Jean trusted Christ as her Savior when she was very young at a Child Evangelism Club in her neighborhood. As a teen, Jean became active in high school activities and was independent and determined to go her own way until she met my cousin Tim. I then met Jean and have a vivid picture of this vibrant, beautiful young lady with long, flowing black hair and a gorgeous smile. Shortly thereafter she became a beautiful bride, pastor's wife, and adoptive mother of two adorable boys about two years apart.

When the boys were in second grade and kindergarten, Jean became desperately ill and landed in the hospital. A few minutes after Jean was given the devastating diagnosis of multiple sclerosis, my uncle came into her hospital room and remembers Jean's response: "I wonder how the Lord is going to use this." Within minutes, the Lord was already using her situation, as her roommate questioned her on how she could be so calm with such a devastating forecast. Jean then was able to give her testimony of her faith in Christ and her assurance that God would take care of her.

The more debilitated her life became, the more Jean continued to see how God was taking care of her every step. When she was first confined to her home, she didn't let that stop her: she began a counseling ministry via her telephone. When she no longer could run and play with her grandchildren, Jean used her electric wheelchair and let them ride with her. Later, when her pain became overbearing, she went to Mayo Clinic for pain therapy. Therapy was hard and strenuous, yet Jean was able to maintain her cheerful attitude in spite of the fact she wanted to quit several times. As a result of her therapy, today she is able to transfer herself from the wheelchair to a chair or a bed on her own.

Jean has learned to accept the fact that the pain is here to stay, but with God she can handle her pain. She has determined that whatever the Lord asks of her, Christ will strengthen her for the task. Jean is known by my family for such a sweet disposition that she spreads sunshine and God's love to everyone who comes near her. Regardless of her challenging physical condition, Jean is still the vibrant, beautiful lady that I remember from many years ago. I believe Jean is a positive influence in many lives because she daily strives to wear the hat of humbleness of mind.

In order to have humbleness of mind, one must have a consciousness of one's defects or shortcomings, not be proud or self-assertive, and show modesty toward self. Humility is one of the supernatural results of being rightly related to God.

Charles Spurgeon says the following:

> When God intends to fill a soul with His Spirit, He first makes it empty;
> When He intends to enrich a soul, He first makes it poor.
> When He intends to exalt a soul, He first makes it sensible of its own miseries, wants, and nothingness.
> I believe every Christian has a choice between being humble or being humbled.[30]

## CHRIST'S HUMILITY

My cousin Jean has learned through her physical limitations that God has to be in control of her life and through Him only she can do the tasks God has for her to accomplish. Jean has to humbly ask for help in areas we so easily take for granted every day. By understanding the humility of Christ, we too can add to our wardrobe the hat of humbleness of mind.

After the humbling of his own virgin birth, Christ subjected Himself to persecution, was treated as a criminal, and was killed by one of the cruelist, most excruciating, and degrading forms of death ever created. Christ lived a life of selfless service and humility that was exemplified by His death on the cross.

1.    In the following verses, list how Christ is described.

Isaiah 53:7

Zechariah 9:9

Matthew 11:29

John 13:5

Philippians 2:8

## Biblical Examples of Humility

The Bible gives us several examples of humility in both the Old Testament and the New Testament. We will look at two: Moses and John the Baptist.

2.  **Moses**

    - According to Hebrews 11:24–26, what was Moses willing to give up?

    - What did Moses feel was most important?

3.  **John the Baptist** (John 1:6–35)

    - What were the people to understand? (v. 20)

    - What did John explain that he wasn't? (v. 21)

    - What did John explain was his purpose? (v. 23)

    - What does John call Jesus? (v. 29)

    - According to Matthew 11:11, what does Jesus call John?

- According to Luke 1:15, what did the angels prophesy?

- Did John the Baptist have a reason to be proud?

- According to John 3:30, what did John think?

- According to Luke 1:26–45, what was Elizabeth's (John's mother's) response to Mary?

- According to Luke 1:43, what did Elizabeth call Mary?

Even from John's birth, he had observed an example of humility. According to Luke 1:76–80, John's parents were examples of humility and, therefore, taught him humility by example.

## STRIVING FOR HUMBLENESS OF MIND

We need to learn to see sin the way God sees sin. Authentic humility is found in those who practice aggressive confession, thus developing a deep realization of unworthiness to receive God's marvelous grace.[31]

4.  According to Romans 12:3, how are we to think of ourselves?

5.  According to Romans 3:12, we are to acknowledge what?

6.  According to Psalms 139:23–24, what are we to do?

7.  According to Colossians 2:7, what are we to be?

8.  According to Acts 17:28, what should we keep in mind?

Remember that God gives us all things. There is nothing to boast about because we didn't receive anything on our own merit.

9. According to Galatians 5:13, what are we to do for others?


How do we do that?


10. According to Matthew 2:11, how did the Magi show their humility?


11. According to Proverbs 31:30, how are we to treat God?


12. According to Proverbs 3:7, what are we to do?


Physical posture can have great impact on spiritual stature. Humility always produces submission to God's divine will and always gives up its own perceived rights. Humility means a right estimation of self and a right understanding of dependence on God.[32]

## THE DANGERS OF PRIDE

Pride always attempts to overcome evil with evil and imagines such a response is justified. Our pride doesn't allow us to put aside our own feelings for the good of others or the furtherance of God's kingdom. If one is stubbornly refusing to admit one's own sin and cannot see any fault except the faults of others, know they are blinded with pride and in danger of its terrible consequences. We need to make a deliberate decision to cultivate humility, the counterpart to pride, beginning with confessing the sin of pride, asking God for a humble heart, and studying everything the Bible has to say about humility.[33]

13. Define *pride*.

14. In the following verses, list the dangers of pride.

    Proverbs 6:16–17

    Proverbs 11:2

    Proverbs 13:10

    Proverbs 16:18

Proverbs 21:4

Proverbs 28:25

Proverbs 29:23

## RESULTS OF HUMILITY

15. In the following verses, list the results of humility.

2 Chronicles 7:14

2 Chronicles 34:27

Proverbs 3:34

Proverbs 6:3

Proverbs 11:2

Proverbs 22:4

James 4:6

James 4:10

1 Peter 5:6

## QUESTIONS TO PONDER

- Do I accept my defects and shortcomings?

- Do I strive to not be self-assertive?

- Do I show modesty toward myself?

- Do I wear the humbleness of mind in my Christian wardrobe?

- **Am I wearing Christ?**

# Lesson 6: The Classic Purse of Meekness

*"Put on therefore ... Meekness"* (Colossians 3:10).

The purse dates back to the fourteenth century when the lady wanted to carry precious items around with her instead of leaving the items behind. We should always include the precious purse of meekness in our wardrobe and carry it with us at all times.

Walter, only known to me as my Uncle Wally, is a quiet, gentle soul, unloved as a child and having never experienced the joy of children or animals. He was always considerate and respectful of others, never had a cross word for anyone, and always showed tremendous love and respect for the Lord, his wife, and other people.

One day Uncle Wally received a phone call from the hospital that his wife had been in a tragic accident. He drove furiously to the hospital only to find his wife had died, and he had lost his very best friend. Overcome with grief and disoriented, he was hospitalized in a mental ward. After many legal challenges and much heartache my parents were able to receive Uncle Wally into their care and through medical experts determined my precious uncle was suffering from Alzheimer's.

Under my parents' care, we watched him as he would enjoy the petting of my dog, raking my dad's lawn every day, watching chipmunks eat his box of crackers, enjoying a s'more for the first time, counting the deluge of deer running through the yard every day, and keeping track of lunchtime.

But at the same time, we also watched Uncle Wally slowly give up his precious memories of his wife, independence of driving a car, carrying a wallet, and living alone—all without complaint.

Later Uncle Wally was moved to a Christian nursing care facility where he is now the apple of everyone's eye. Over ten years have passed since Uncle Wally arrived at this caring facility, and they fear his time is short. The nurses and residents have asked that when the Lord takes him home, they could have a special memorial service at the facility because so many medical staff and residents are attached to this precious man—the quiet, gentle soul. My Uncle Wally is a true example of a lifetime of meekness.

*Meekness* in Greek is called *praotes* (prah-oo-tace), which means mild or gentle.[34] In James 1:21, we are told to "receive with meekness," in James 3:13 we are told about the "meekness of wisdom," and in 1 Peter 3:15 we are told to "be ready to give an answer ... with meekness."

## Christ's Meekness

Jesus Christ who became the sacrificial lamb for our sins on the cross uttered no protest against the oppressors. When Jesus was arrested in Luke 23:9 he answered King Herod nothing. In Matthew 26:63 Jesus held his peace when he was indicted. According to Matthew 27:12 when Jesus was accused, he answered nothing.

> Christ also suffered for us, leaving us an example that ye should follow his steps. Who did no sin, neither was guile found in his mouth. Who when he was reviled, reviled not again; when he suffered he threatened not but committed himself to him that judgeth righteously (1 Peter 2:21b-23).

## Striving for Meekness

Meekness is a result of a strong man's choice to control his reactions in submission to God. It is a balance born of strength of character, stemming from confident trust in God, not from weakness or fear.[35] The meek person has his instincts, impulses, and passions under the control of God.[36] Our choice to control our reactions and obtain that gentle, quiet spirit can be learned through teachers, donkeys, or circumstances.

## Through Teachers

Our teachability most often depends on our teacher. If we respect the teacher, we might accept the teaching.[37]

1. In Acts 18:24–28, what was Apollo willing to do?

2. According to James 1:21–22, what are we to do?

As you read Numbers 22:2–20, consider the following thought: if we don't respect the teacher, then God might send a donkey.

## THROUGH DONKEYS

In Numbers 22, we find a story about Balaam who was considered a false prophet. He practiced magic and witchcraft and made money from his gift.

The Moabites were descendants of Lot, and Balak their king had seen how the Israelites had the destroyed the Amorites. Balak was terrified the same thing would happen to the Moabites.

The Midianites, descendants of Abraham, joined in alliance with the Moabites to defeat Israel. However, Balak knew the Israelites were still too strong militarily, so the Midianites went to Balaam. They wanted Balaam to go with them and pronounce a curse on the Israelites.

Balaam goes to his gods for "advice." However, Jehovah God intervenes and tells him the Israelites are a blessed people and he is not to go and cast a spell. Balaam is tempted to do it anyway because it would bring him great honor. God tells him he can go, but Balaam must only speak what God wants him to say. Balaam went with the Moabites regardless of God's instruction to speak God's words only. Therefore, Balaam disrespected God and went with the Moabites with the wrong motive in mind.

3.  Answer the following verses using Numbers 22:21–38.

    • What did the donkey see and do, and how did Balaam react? (v. 23)

    • What did the donkey do next, and what did Balaam do? (v. 25)

    • Where did the angel stand, and what did the donkey do? (v. 26)

    • What did Balaam do? (v. 27)

    • According to verse twenty-eight, after the third beating, what did God do with the donkey?

    • Why did God oppose Balaam? (v. 32)

---

- If the donkey had continued and not turned away from the angel, what would have happened? (v. 33)

When we are proud, rebellious, and insist on our own way, the chances are good that God will use a donkey. These unlikely teachers have a two-fold purpose of bringing humility and instruction. Often we will learn no other way.[38] Sometimes we don't mind something new; we just don't like the vehicle God is using to drive us to a new place.[39] The precious part of *praotes* is being willing and anxious to learn, regardless of whom He chooses as our unlikely teacher or donkey. If, however, we don't learn through teachers or donkeys, we might have to learn through circumstances.

## THROUGH CIRCUMSTANCES

In the story of the Ark of the Covenant, we find in Exodus 25:13–15 that the ark was built with staves (poles) that were made of shittim wood covered in gold and inserted in rings. That was how the ark was to be transported. In Numbers 1:50–52, we see the instruction also that the Levites were in charge of the tabernacle and would "bear" the tabernacle. In 1 Chronicles 13, David has a desire to bring the Ark of the Covenant home to Jerusalem.

4. In 1 Chronicles 13:7–14, describe what happened.

*David wanted maximum results with minimum instruction.*[40]

5. In 1 Chronicles 15:14–15, what did David do?

6. What causes us to keep God's word? (Psalms 119:67)

7. What causes us to learn God's statutes? (Psalms 119:71)

We miss one of the most crucial purposes of difficult circumstances if we don't accept them as invitations to get into God's Word.[41]

8. Why should we lay up God's Word in our heart? (Proverbs 4:13)

9. What happens if we respect God's commandments? (Proverbs 13:13)

To miss God's Word in our circumstances is to miss God. To miss God is to miss the point.[42]

## QUESTIONS TO PONDER

- Am I easy to approach, even about difficult matters?

- Do others have legitimate reasons to dread conversations with me?

- Do I endure misunderstandings and injustice without retaliating or being defensive?

- Do I have a yielding and teachable spirit?[43] Do I have a willingness to learn, am I compliant, am I willing to step out of my comfort zone and learn something new?

- Do I carry the classic purse of meekness with me wherever I go? **Do I wear Christ?**

# Lesson 7: The Pearls of Longsuffering

*"Put on therefore ... longsuffering,
forbearing one another, and forgiving
one another"* (Colossians 3:12–13).

Pearls have been a favorite gem since ancient times. Their appeal is universal. For centuries pearls have been a treasure of almost incomparable value. A pearl necklace adds elegance and sophistication to any occasion and is actually formed from an irritant that enters the oyster. Pearls of longsuffering are essential to the Christian wardrobe. Longsuffering is that finishing detail that will give you that polished look.

My friend and I as teenagers went on our annual trek of picking wild blackberries. But one day we decided to take my dad's pickup truck and drive to the berry patches because we just had a rainstorm and we didn't want to get muddy and wet. Well the berry patches were located in a very boggy part of Skare Park, and I proceeded to drive right to the area where the wild blackberry bushes were located, and—yep, you guessed it—the pickup got stuck. The truck was so badly stuck that the axles of the truck were nowhere in sight. I knew we had to hike back to my house (no cell phones in those days) and tell my dad the horrible news and ask him to come and save his truck. My dad, with no other reaction, said, "Come on, let's go get my truck out of the mud." My dad stopped what he was doing and we dutifully rode over to the area where the truck was located. My dad took one look at the truck and promptly replied, "Yep, it's stuck." Miracle of miracles, another truck pulled the pickup truck right out. Dad even let me drive the truck out of the area and let me and my friend continue on with our fun in the park. (However, I think we were out of the mood for picking wild blackberries). My dad never spoke about that event other than maybe make fun of me a few times. My dad has always shown such longsuffering to me even when my brain light bulb isn't plugged in or is plugged in and not working very well.

Longsuffering is synonymous with forbearance, which means to endure, put up with, and show patience for the errors or weaknesses of anyone.[44] Synonymous with forbearance is patience or endurance (*makrothumia*) with people, slowness in avenging wrongs.[45]

In Ephesians 4:2, we are told "with longsuffering, forbearing one another in love." Longsuffering is also synonymous with tolerance and gentleness.[46] We are called to deal with frustrating people. Convenience never produces character, but irritants do.

## God's Longsuffering

God has been striving to call people to repentance and righteousness since the first sin was committed in the garden of Eden. God has tremendous capacity for patience before he breaks through in judgment. God endures endless blasphemies against his name while waiting for people to be saved.

The Lord is not slack concerning his promise, as some men count slackness, but is longsuffering to us-ward, not willing that any should perish but that all should come to repentance (2 Peter 3:9).

1. In Genesis 6:5, how were the people described?

2. In Genesis 6:3, how long was God's warning?

3. According to Lamentations 3:22–23, when does God's mercy end?

4. In 1 Peter 3:20, with whom is God being patient?

5. In 2 Peter 2:5, how is Noah described? Were there any true converts?

6. In 2 Peter 3:9, who is God longsuffering with?

## Practicing Longsuffering

If we're going to become vessels of God's patience toward others, we must learn to be void of judgment toward others.[47] Judgment strangles *makrothumia* and grieves the Holy Spirit. We can't both judge others and be patient toward them. One cancels out the other.

7. What happens when we condemn others? (Romans 2:1–5)

8. If God's judgment is based on truth, what is ours based on?

9. Our judgment of others means we have what feelings about God's judgment? Is our judgment purely righteous?

10. If we judge others, what may happen to us? (Matthew 7:1–5)

11. Our judgment of others is hindered by what?

12. Who only has the right to judge? (James 4:11–12)

13. What standard do we use when we judge? What standard does God use? (John 8:14–18)

## APPLY LESSONS LEARNED

We can't love God when we are not willing to love his children, even when they are not very lovable.

14. What does longsuffering do for us? (James 1:2–4)

15. Forbearing with people can bring out the worst in us. But according to Ephesians 4:2 and Romans 12:3, what does forbearance with people do for us?

The word *moderation* in Philippians 4:5 is the word used for gentle or patient. It is synonymous with the following:

- forbearance (*makrothumia*)[48]

- patience (*hupomone*)[49]

- gentleness (*praotes*)[50]

- tolerance (*anoche*)[51]

A Christian should be characterized as one who is gentle and forbearing toward others, and one who makes reasonable demands.

## QUESTIONS TO PONDER

- Am I gentle and patient toward others?

- Do I wait patiently?

- Am I reasonable in my demands of others?

- Am I willing to love those who are unlovable?

- Do I possess the pearls of longsuffering?

- **Do I wear Christ?**

# Lesson 8: The Earrings of Peace

*"And let the peace of God rule in your hearts*
*... and be ye thankful"* (Colossians 3:15).

Earrings were designed to enhance your face and make you sparkle and shine. The earrings of peace are an essential part of our Christian wardrobe, because they enhance our Christian life and make us sparkle and shine regardless of the situation. Peace means a quietness or tranquility despite the storm that may surround us. Believers have an attitude of rest and security because of that eternal peace in their life.[52]

My first memories of my cousin Christopher (technically my first cousin once removed) were of an adorable fair-skinned, redheaded little boy at my uncle's cabin on the lake. The family was all together visiting, playing, and enjoying lakefront activities; my aunt and uncle were busily preparing a huge meal for all of us; and little Chris was sitting quietly at the picnic table waiting anxiously for those hot dogs to roll off my uncle's grill and right onto his plate.

Chris was saved at five years old, grew up in a Christian home, and went to church all of his life. The next thing I remember is that Chris had grown into a quiet, gentle giant (I believe too many of my uncle's hot dogs). He was a quiet testimony to all who were around him, and even as a teenager encouraged his friend Josh to get back into church and serve the Lord (Josh later graduated from a Bible college and became a youth pastor).

On May 22, 2006, at age twenty-one, Chris was diagnosed with melanoma cancer. Almost a year from his first doctor's appointment, it was discovered Chris's cancer had spread throughout his whole body, and he was only given a few weeks to live. Chris had many discussions with his pastor during those difficult days. He shared his greatest joy was going home to be with the Lord. His biggest regret was that he had not accomplished much for the Lord. His pastor challenged Chris that he had a more significant ministry now than he could have had with a long life. "You must show us how to die," and Chris determined to do just that.

When family and friends were having trouble with their emotions, Chris showed tremendous peace and calm. Chris used less medicine than was prescribed so that he could stay alert and enjoy his family and friends as long as possible, and yet he still provided humor even while in tremendous pain. Chris's pastor described him as one who was faithful in adversity, never cursed God, and never forsook his maker.

Chris left the hospital to enjoy his last days in his parents' home. After he came home, Chris was found sobbing in agony of soul, and his pastor asked him, "Chris, is it hard because you've come home to die?" Chris said, "No, it is because I'm not home and I want to go home." On July 4, 2007, at age twenty-two, Christopher finally got to go home. Christopher is one of the best examples I know of wearing the peace of God even in the midst of tremendous adversity.

We can't wear the wardrobe item of the peace *of* God until we have peace *with* God. [53] Chris, early on in his life, obtained peace with God by accepting Christ as his Savior. Chris then could enjoy the peace of God even during turbulent times.

## THE PEACE OF GOD

In Isaiah 9:6, God is called the "Prince of Peace." God's peace is paramount to spiritual, mental, and emotional wholeness[54] Man cannot create peace in his own soul.[55] Those who have inner peace and are rejoicing in the Lord have a predisposition to harmony with other Christians.[56]

1.  Below list what happens as a result of God's peace in our lives.

   John 14:27

   Romans 15:33

Ephesians 2:14

Philippians 4:9

1 Thessalonians 5:23

Hebrews 13:20–21

In Matthew 14:22–36, we find Peter switched his focus to his circumstances while Christ remained tightly focused on His destination.[57] The peace of God ruled in my cousin Chris's life because he stayed focused on his destination and not on his present circumstances.

2.  In the following passage of Scripture, John 11:1–44, describe the scene.

• About what was Jesus being notified?

• How did Jesus react?

• When Jesus decided to go to Bethany, how did the disciples react?

- Who met Jesus on the way to Bethany?

- What happened when Mary went to meet Jesus?

- What did Jesus do at that meeting?

- How did the scene end?

Christ experienced peace in the midst of tears. Peace means the absence of fear and turmoil, not the absence of pain and grief.[58]

## Obtain God's Peace

"Those who are at peace with themselves have a proper platform on which to build a relationship of peace and harmony with others. Too often inner friction results in outer friction. Keeping peace in the heart will help keep peace in the church."[59] The peace of God can be obtained by prayer, studying God's word, and having a thankful heart.

## Prayer

3. According to Philippians 4:6–9, what happens when we pray with supplication and thanksgiving?

## STUDY THE BIBLE

4.   In Luke 1:46–47, what response did Mary have even though there was a big question mark in her life?

5.   What does God's Word promise us in Isaiah 26:3?

## BE THANKFUL

George Matheson was a blind preacher of Scotland. One time after he had become blind, he prayed, "My God, I have not thanked thee for my thorn. I have thanked thee 1,000 times for my roses. Teach me the value of my thorn."[60]

6.   According to 1 Thessalonians 5:18, what is God's will for us?

7.   In Ephesians 5:20, how is our process of thankfulness described?

8. According to Proverbs 15:15, what does thankfulness do for us?

Thankfulness allows us to see the light side of every circumstance. Always strive to look for the potential good that God will cause to come out of adversity rather than the present adversity itself.

## QUESTIONS TO PONDER

- When I am under pressure, is my spirit generally calm rather than frantic or turbulent?

- Do I exhibit an inner tranquility of mind and a quiet confidence that God is in control, regardless of what is going on around me?

- Do quietness and tranquility pervade my character even when I am in the midst of a storm?

- Do I wear the earrings of peace with me? **Do I wear Christ?**

# Lesson 9: The Coat of Charity

*"And above all these things put on charity, which is the bond of perfectness"* (Colossians 3:14*).*

The timeless trench coat is a stylish outer garment that covers you and protects you and will take you from season to season. The timeless trench coat of love covers you, protects you, and is essential for the Christian wardrobe. Love is a **demonstration**, not an inclination. There is involvement, movement, expression.[61]

Love (*agape*) is an act of the will toward an unconditional expression of love. Agape love doesn't just verbalize, but **mobilizes into action**. It is **something you do for someone**.[62]

Love is ...

- My husband traveling forty minutes one way to bring me a single rose to my office "just because" and having a meal and a fire in the fireplace ready after a long day at my job on a long winter's eve.

- My mom trudging a quarter of a mile through the woods in two feet of snow, bringing me her homemade chicken soup when I don't feel good and stopping her busy daily routine to have a cup of tea with me when I stop by unexpectedly to say, "Hi."

- My dad plowing our driveway unexpectedly after a major blizzard and leaving his homegrown produce at our door.

- My twenty-something niece making me a beautiful memorial plaque of my precious dog Kerrie and driving eight hundred miles one way to give it to me in person.

- My WOW Sunday school class giving such great hugs, notes, and words of encouragement when I need them most.

- A precious lady in my church, enduring much personal affliction, sending me a priceless note in the mail when I need it the most.

- Our spoiled-rotten dog Rocky coming by my side of the bed every night and touching my hand to tell me good night.

## GOD'S LOVE REVEALED

In John 12:1–3, we find the story of Mary of Bethany washing Jesus's feet. Mary used a pound of oil of spikenard, which was an oil extracted from the root of a plant grown in India. In verse five of John 12, we find that the ointment was worth about a year's wages.[63] Mary's treasure was not in her trousseau. Her hope didn't lie in what she could get from Jesus. Her joy lay in what she could give.[64] Mary's motive was pure because she loved Jesus with her whole heart and wanted nothing in return. The following are three areas where Jesus demonstrated his unconditional love to others.

## JESUS WAS AVAILABLE

1.  List to whom Jesus was made available.

    Matthew 8:28–34

    Mark 9:27–31

    Luke 8:40–56

    Luke 10:38–42

## JESUS WENT OUT OF HIS WAY

2.  In Matthew 14:14, Jesus just found out his cousin John had just been executed days before. Jesus wanted to be alone. But what happened?

## JESUS SERVED

3.  In the following Scripture passages, describe how Jesus was serving.

    John 13:5

    John 21:6–12

    Mark 14:3–8

    Luke 14:1–4

## PRACTICING GOD'S LOVE

4.  According to 1 John 4:7–12, why are we to practice God's love?

5.  How can I demonstrate love to others, especially to those who are unlovable?

## Questions to Ponder

- Am I always available for others without expecting anything in return?

- Do I go out of the way for others without expecting anything in return?

- Do I serve others and not for my own glory?

- Do people genuinely know that I love them and will help them in any way that I can, or do they think I have a selfish motive for helping them?

- Do I genuinely love those people in my life who are unlovable or who do not love me in return?

**What is charity?**
**It is silence, when your words would hurt.**
**It is patience, when your neighbor's curt.**
**It is deafness, when a scandal flows.**
**It is thoughtfulness, for other's woes.**
**It is promptness, when a duty calls.**
**It is courage, when misfortune falls. (Unknown)**

# Lesson 10: The Power of the Holy Spirit

*"Let the word of Christ dwell in you richly in all wisdom, teaching and admonishing one another in psalm and hymns and spiritual songs, singing with grace in your hearts to the Lord. And whatsoever ye do in word or deed, do all in the name of the Lord Jesus, giving thanks to God and the Father by him" Colossians 3:16–17).*

After Jesus's resurrection from the dead, the disciples had a very hard time understanding what had happened. They struggled with the accounts they had heard that Jesus had risen from the grave. Peter even had to go to the tomb himself to check it out—and sure enough there was no body.

One day while the disciples were talking together and hearing about another firsthand account of an appearance of Jesus after the resurrection, Jesus appeared in their midst and the disciples were terrified until they realized who He was. As He talked with the disciples around a meal, Jesus explained the great commission and that "repentance and remission of sins should be preached in His name among all nations, beginning at Jerusalem."

You can just imagine the disciples' conversation with Jesus.

- What do you want us to do, Lord?

- When do we get started?

- Let's draft a master plan and get started.

- James and John can get started on a mission statement.

- Peter needs to work out a ten-year strategy.

- Matthew needs to run some numbers to see how much money we will need.

- Lord, when do you want us to begin? People have to hear what we have witnessed!

However, Jesus replied by telling the disciples they must wait. They are to stay in Jerusalem until Jesus sends them the "promise of the Father upon you."

Jesus then ascended to heaven and the disciples continued worshiping Jesus and waiting for the promise. Jesus knew that the disciples needed the power of the Holy Spirit in their life, or everything they did would be in vain.

On the day of the celebration of Pentecost, the Holy Spirit (the promise) did come, news spread about what had happened, Peter was able to preach his first gospel sermon, and the people listening were convicted of their sin, were saved, and were baptized—almost three thousand people.

Although there will always be some lingering influence of the flesh until we meet the Lord, we have no excuse for allowing sin to continue to corrupt our lives ... "We have the resources of the Spirit of Christ within us to resist and put to death the deeds of the body, which result from living according to the flesh"[65]

The same Godhead in Genesis 1:1–2 that had the power to bring the world into existence is the same power that we have in us as Christians. We have everything we need by the Holy Spirit living in us.

## ACTIVITY OF THE HOLY SPIRIT

The Comforter is described as an advocate, intercessor, and one who pleads the cause of anyone before a judge, one who bestows spiritual aid and consolation.[66]

1.  Describe the Holy Spirit using the following Scripture passages.

    1 Corinthians 3:16

    Psalms 139:7–12

    Ezekiel 36:27

Acts 1:8


Romans 5:5


Romans 15:13


1 Corinthians 12:4–11


Galatians 5:22–23


John 16:7–11


John 6:63


John 14:26

## Victory with the Holy Spirit

According to Galatians 5:16, "Walk in the Spirit, and ye shall not fulfill the lust of the flesh." *Walk* is a present imperative, a command to do something in the future, and involves **continuous** or **repeated** action.

One of our biggest reasons for failure in daily struggles is our vain (empty) attempt to balance the Holy Spirit and the flesh (old nature, flesh woman)— to make them function as coworkers. It is absolutely impossible. They cannot work together because they are polar opposites. [67]

## Steps to a Spirit-Filled Life

When we are saved, we enter a process called sanctification. Sanctification is defined as the progressive work of God that frees us from sin's control and makes us more like Christ.[68] The process of being sanctified isn't easy. Some of our enemies are external, such as Satan and the world. However, there is also an internal war of enemies in our heart between the old man and the new man.

> For the flesh lusteth against the Spirit, and the Spirit against the flesh and these are contrary the one to the other, so that ye cannot do the things that ye would (Galatians 5:17).

The Holy Spirit gives us as Christians the desire to be free from the control of sin. The pull of the flesh is strong but the Spirit is even more powerful. We must apply faith in the power of the indwelling Holy Spirit to grant us victory over the flesh.

The following are four steps toward a spirit-filled life.

### Step 1: Put to death the sin in our life

Colossians 3:5–8 tells us to put to the death the sins that are in our body.

    1.    According to 1 John 1:9, how are we to put to death that sin that is in our body?

    2.    When we put that sin to death, what does God do with our sin? (Psalms 103:12)

### Step 2: Spend time in God's Word

We need to learn to build a relationship with God. A close relationship doesn't come automatically; it takes time, energy, and nurturing. Colossians 3:16 tells us to "let the Word of Christ dwell in you richly in all wisdom." Therefore, God's Word is to be abundantly at home in our hearts. The Scripture should permeate every aspect of the believer's life and control every thought, word, and deed.[69]

3.   According to Matthew 4:4, how important is God's Word to us?

4.   1 Peter 2:2–3 says the Bible helps us with what?

5.   According to Romans 10:7, what develops as a result of hearing the Word of God?

6.   Because we are continually building a relationship with God, what does Psalms 119:11 say it will do for us to study God's Word?

7.   For the Scripture to become profitable for us, what must we do? (2 Timothy 2:15)

8. If we carry out number six, what does the Scripture do for us? (Acts 20:32)

9. List two things that God's Word does for us? (Joshua 1:8)

The filling of the Holy Spirit is a steady, controlling life through the obedience of God's Word. Your submission to God begins by reading his Word and by applying it to your everyday life. Submission to God is letting God's Word begin to enrich your life. Having God in your everyday life is not a duty but a relationship that you are building. (You typically spend time only with those with whom you want a relationship.)

**Step 3: Fill our hearts with Song**

Colossians 3:16 tells us to "teach and admonish one another in psalms, hymns, and spiritual songs." This means singing songs not only in public but also in private. Because the Lord is the source and object of our song, singing is worshiping the Lord.

10. According to the following verses, why is it important to sing praises?

Psalms 33:1

Psalms 40:3


Acts 16:25


**Step 4: Be Thankful**

Colossians 3:17 tells us that whatever we do, "give thanks to God and the Father."

11.  1 Thessalonians 5:18 tells us what about being thankful?


Being thankful is an indication of submission to Him and the key that unlocks the Spirit-filled life.[70]

## QUESTIONS TO PONDER

- Do I spend time in God's Word?

- Do I fill my heart with songs praising God?

- Do I have a thankful heart?

- Am I utilizing the power of the Holy Spirit in my life?

- What wardrobe am I more consistently wearing? The following are contrasting pairs. Place a check mark next to the one that most often characterizes your life.

| WARDROBE OF OLD NATURE | WARDROBE OF NEW NATURE |
|---|---|
| Strict, severe, unkind | Merciful, tolerant |
| Impatient, selfish, unfriendly | Kind, tender |
| Boastful, overbearing, | Humble, modest |
| Demanding, jealous, | Meek, gentle, friendly |
| Impatient | Longsuffering, patient |
| Gossip and judgment , Hateful or hate-filled | Peaceful, tranquil, loving |

The degree of change in the Christian life will be in direct proportion to that person's yielding to the Holy Spirit.[71] Remember, even though we received the Holy Spirit in our heart at the point of salvation, that doesn't mean we have given Him permission to rule in every area of our heart and life. We have areas of our heart that are still holding on to our old thoughts, ways, and actions and we are not willing to give them up and yield to the Holy Spirit and let Him take control.

They that wait upon the Lord, shall renew their strength; they shall mount up with wings as eagles; they shall run and not be weary; they shall walk and not faint. Isaiah 40:30.

# Bibliography

*A Tale of Two Sisters.* Camp Joy, Whitewater, Wisconsin, Whitewater, 1985.

George, Elizabeth. *A Woman after God's Own Heart.* Eugene, Oregon, Harvest House Publishers, 1984.

Grissom, Nancy Leigh, and Grissom, Tim. *Seeking Him: Experiencing the Joy of Personal Revival.* Chicago, Illinois, Moody Publishers, 2004.

Halley, Henry. H. *Halley's Bible Handbook, NIV,* Grand Rapids, Michigan, Zondervan, 2007.

Jones, Beneth. *Beauty and the Best: A Handbook of Christian Loveliness.* Greenville, South Carolina, Bob Jones University, 1980.

Moore, Beth. *Living Beyond Yourself: Exploring the Fruit of the Spirit.* Nashville, Tennessee, Lifeway Press, 2004.

Nelson, Ed. *Growing in Grace.* Denver, Colorado, Mile High Publishers, 1991.

Pryde, Debi. *Secrets of a Happy Heart: Titus 2 Series-Book 1.* Newberry Springs, California, Iron Sharpeneth Iron Publications, 2002.

Ryrie, Charles. *The Ryrie Study Bible, KJV.* Chicago, Illinois, Moody Press, 1978.

Stamm, Millie. *Be Still and Know.* Grand Rapids, Michigan, Zondervan Books, 1978.

Swindoll, Charles. *Dropping Your Guard: The Value of Open Relationships.* Waco, Texas, World Books Publishers, 1983.

Timmons, Tim. *Stress in the Family: How to Live through It.* Eugene, Oregon, Harvest House Publishers, 1982.

Weaver, Joanna. *Having a Mary Heart in a Martha World: Finding Intimacy with God in the Business of Life.* Colorado      Springs, Colorado, Waterbrook Press, 2000.

Wiersbe, Warren. *Waiting on God in Difficult Times.* Wheaton, Illinois, Victor Books, 1984.

Wolvoord, John. *Philippians: Triumph in Christ.* Chicago, Illinois, Moody Bible Institue, 1971.

Zodhiates, Spiros. *Hebrew-Greek Key Word Study Bible: Key Insights into God's Word.* Chattanooga, Tennessee, AMG Publishers, 2008.

# Endnotes

1.  Beneth Jones. *Beauty and the Best: A Handbook of Christian Loveliness.* Greenville, South Carolina, Bob Jones University Press, 1980, p. 3.

2.  *A Tale of Two Sisters. Whitewater,* Wisconsin, Camp Joy, p. 1,985.

3.  *Zodhiates*, p. 1,585.

4.  Ibid. p. 193.

5.  Ibid. p. 42.

6.  Ibid. p. 229.

7.  Weaver, p. 14.

8.  *Zodhiates*, p. 2,062.

9.  Ibid. p. 2062.

10. Jones, p. 104.

11. Charles Ryrie, *The Ryrie Study Bible, KJV.* Chicago, Moody Press, 1978, p. 1,694.

12. Ed Nelson, *Growing in Grace,* Denver, Colorado, Mile High Publishers, 1991, p. 65.

13. *Zodhiates*, p. 1,654.

14. Dunn, p. 64.

15. *Zodhiates*, p. 1,217.

16. Ibid., p. 70.

17. Elizabeth George. *A Woman after God's Own Heart.* Eugene, Oregon, Harvest House Publishers, 1984, p. 239.

18. Charles Swindoll. *Dropping Your Guard: The Value of Open Relationships.* Waco, Texas, World Books Publishers, 1983, p. 139.

19. George, p. 70.

20. Ibid., p. 32.

21. Ibid., p. 129.

22. Ibid., p. 128.

23. *Zodhiates*, 5,544.

24. Beth Moore. *Living beyond Yourself: Exploring the Fruit of the Spirit.* Nashville, Tennessee, Lifeway Press, 2004, p. 5.

25. Warren Wiersbe. *Be Patient: Waiting on God in Difficult Times.* Wheaton, Illinois, Victor Books, 1984, p. 61.

26. Ibid.

27. *Zodhiates*, 5,544.

28. Moore, p. 146.

29. Moore, p. 136.

30. Pryde, p. 28.

31. Moore, p. 183.

32. Debi Pryde. *Secrets of a Happy Heart: Titus 2 Series, Book 1.* Newberry Springs, California, Iron Sharpeneth Iron Publications, 2002, p. 27.

33. Pryde, p. 135.

34. *Zodhiates*, p. 2,225.

35. Ibid.

36. Dunn, p. 37.

37. Moore, p. 187.

38. Ibid., p. 188.

39. Ibid., p. 189.

40. Ibid., p. 191.

41. Ibid., p. 192.

42. Ibid., p. 193.

43.  Nancy Leigh Demoss and Tim Grissom. *Seeking Him: Experiencing the Joy of Personal Revival.* Chicago, Moody Publishers, 2004, p. 231.

44.  *Zodhiates*, p. 430.

45.  Ibid., p. 315.

46.  Ibid., p. 463 and p. 1,932.

47.  Moore, p. 123.

48.  *Zodhiates*, p. 3,115.

49.  Ibid., p. 5,281.

50.  Ibid., p. 4,236.

51.  Ibid., p. 463.

52.  MacArthur, p. 1,743.

53.  Moore, p. 100.

54.  Ibid. p. 98.

55.  Ibid. p. 97.

56.  John Wolvoord. *Philippians: Triumph in Christ.* Chicago, Illinois, Moody Bible Institute, 1971, p. 108.

57.  Moore, p. 105.

58.  Ibid., p. 107.

59.  Wolvoord, p. 108.

60. Millie Stamm. *Be Still and Know.* Grand Rapids, Michigan, Zondervan Books, 1978.

61. Charles Swindoll. *Dropping Your Guard: The Value of Open Relationships.* Waco, Texas, Word Books Publishers, 1983, p. 121.

62. Tim Timmons. *Stress in the Family: How to Live Through It.* Eugene, Oregon, Harvest House Publishers, 1982, p. 108.

63. McArthur, p. 1,398.

64. Joanna Weaver, *Having a Mary Heart in a Martha World: Finding Intimacy with God in the Business of Life.* Colorado Springs, Colorado, Waterbrook Press, 2000, p. 164.

65. Ibid., p. 224.

66. *Zodhiates*, p. 2,210.

67. Moore, p. 43.

68. Demoss, p. 222.

69. McArthur, p. 1,743.

70. LaHaye, p. 218.

71. LaHaye, p. 231.